Like A Leaf Love The Sun

Robert Wildwood

Printed in the USA 2023

This book is dedicated to
Henry Hydrangea
Loyal, Loving, Fierce, Beautiful.
We will always love you.

Thank you to
the League of Minnesota Poets:
Duluth Poetry Chapter for endless
inspiration and support. Your passion
bravely shared with strangers has been
inspiration and a light to me.

These poems were written and shared on ancestral land of the indigenous Anishinaabe people who still live and thrive here while protecting the living land as they have done for thousands of years.

We oppose the colonialism, white supremacy, and genocide which indigenous people have resisted on these lands for more than 500 years.

Like A Leaf Love The Sun
table of contents

8. One World
9. This Pen
10. If I Carry The Light
11. My Birthday Is Your Birthday
12. Super Chill Toddler Soccer
13. Ecstatic One Block Walk
14. Crinkly Wrapper Toddler Summoning
15. Sitting On The Steps She Surprises Me
16. Grandpa Alec Said If You Point Your Finger At Someone You Have Three More Fingers Pointing Back At You
17. Simple Terms
18. Forces Of Flow
20. Visions In The Mirror
22. Peekaboo We See You
23. Strange That We Get Up And Go To Work
24. Henry Earns A Biscuit
27. Time Reveals
28. Everything Will Change No Way To Explain
29. Adult Lessons Taught By Toddlers
30. The Human Nest Revisited
31. Be Easy On We
32. I See You, Future Me
33. Welcome Fear

34. Water Makes Slippery
35. Our Country Is A Dream
36. Spontaneous Play Wreck A Plan
37. Secrets Of The Baby
38. Welcome To The Wildwoods
39. Seven Chrysalides
40. Stardust Pirate
42. Be Frosty!
44. Mason Jar On Counter
45. Do Butterflies Have Fun
46. Smile All Day
47. The Naked Knock
49. Let's Play Follow The Money
    (first appeared in New Verse News, 2022)
50. Try Good Things
51. Freight Trains In Ireland
53. Truth, Love, Fire
54. Non-Violent Tic-Tac-Toe Solution
55. Do It Every Day
56. A Nurse And The Unknown
57. Choose Wisely
59. Hey Old Dog
61. Butter Side Up
62. Infinity Wave
64. One Month Ago
65. Childhood Energy Flow
66. If I Had A Friend I Would Be Talking
    Not Writing

67. A Multitude Walking As One
68. Do Not Spend The Present In The Future
69. Secret Words Of Power
70. With Respect We Say Sunrise Not Earthspin
71. Fresh Cold Free
72. Together We Walk Into This Night
74. The End Of Time Is The Beginning
77. We Do Not Control This
78. Duluth Is Creeks
79. Reminder
80. First Ballet Night
81. Window Forecast
82. Smiling At Fear
85. Using Ink And Paper To Write So An Artificial Intelligence Cant Hear Me Think
87. Working On Love
88. Thank You For Giving Me Life
91. Broken Door Bad Sign
92. A Cascade of Progressively Optimistic Voices Convinces Me Not to Quit
94. Flying High
95. Changing Everything
97. White People Are A White People Problem
100. Obligatory Stressed Overwhelmed Relaxing Saturday Walk
101. Do Not Run When Crossing
104. This Lake We Drink

105. Always Connected
106. A Burden Lifted
107. Tic-Tac-Toe Revelations
109. Never Waste A Day
110. Honoring Grandmother
111. As I Held You Hold Me Too
112. Neighbors Not Seen
113. Using The Sun To Read
114. Poet Monomaniac
116. Daylight The Creeks
117. The Feeling of Walking In The Dark Down A Path You Have Never Been On
118. Reach Out Now
119. We Too Are Developing
120. Stars On Earth
121. When The Sun Smiles On Us
122. Late April Loon-Fall
124. This Morning I Found
125. Can I Change The World
126. Today I Need To
127. Fun Is Always

one world
many people
we are one

this pen
is not connected
to the
world wide web
this pen is
interconnected
to everything

if i carry the light
with me today
it will be
a good day

My Birthday Is Our Birthday

she is sleeping now
i have one eye on this screen watching
an arm moves a little
wondering if i may soon
abandon this poem for love
she still sleeping
awake i dream
birthday in the park
invite the bell to ring
Japanese bronze the gift
conflict and love
read the sign
human recognition
one
world
feet on smooth bedrock high up
sight of water horizon
feel infinity
somewhere in the distance
here at home
a dog and child are
sleeping on the bed
looks good
i join

Super Chill Toddler Soccer

surrounded by life at Kickstarters Soccer
flying crawling walking growing
we are alive thinking breathing walking
creating consuming
teaching my daughter that
when you eat tasty food
it becomes poop and
she could not believe it
climbing tree the climbing tree
i want to climb there will be climbing
unfiltered toddlers alive climbing
reaching for the sun
soccer balls in all directions
the parachute then
collapsible fabric tunnel crawl becomes
volcano full of soccer ball lava
exploding for them to chase
parents grandparents watch toddler swarm
squeals of joy tears of angst
cookie monster runs and toddlers chase
when they catch her
coach eats all the cookies given
then the air fills with tiny bubbles
tiny hands touch spheres that disappear

Ecstatic One Block Walk

strolling drunk up our street
everything awake and smiling
synapses snapping crackling
dark sky bright by summer lights
tall trees watching laughing
i hold the glass steady
hard rock around
i am fortunate
i remember past and future
puzzle is solved
the smallest code in
microbes and chemical skeletons
okay so this is the matrix
cant really see everything but
i can feel it

Crinkly Wrapper Toddler Summoning

this treat has
power to calm
emotional melt down
when leaving playground
annies homegrown organic
bunny fruit snacks
berry patch flavor
we share this love
we call simply
fruities

Sitting On The Steps She Surprises Me

i saw you reaching for
a play teacup
sitting on the deck railing
later you said to me
I drank what the rain gave me.
You drank rainwater out of your teacup?
Yeah. I was thirsty.
sitting on our front steps you said
Poppa, i'm happy that you're here.
Did you have a good birthday?
Yes. This is the
best birthday ever.
Did you like the cupcakes i made
with momma?
They were delicious yes.
Poppa can you say thank you?
Thank you.
Poppa, i love you.
I love you too.

Grandpa Alec Said If You Point Your Finger At Someone You Have Three More Fingers Pointing Back At You

forsythia flowered for the first time
later the peonies first bloom
new baby due october
big changes and good changes
inside our home and
within property boundaries
news from beyond troubling
religious extremists
control supreme court
pointing fingers
passing judgments
like i do sometimes
before i realize
good thing i'm not
one of those

Simple Terms

we like to think of things in simple terms
easier for us to process
categorize which is useful
dealing with a world full of possibilities
easier to make fast decisions
consolidate community
rally your people
dominate or survive
black and white
guns are not pro life
black lives matter
fire is hot
poor people
will steal your wallet
water is wet
rich people
will steal your
whole paycheck

Forces of Flow

the after work
fifteen minute moment
here at the windows of
Miller Creek Overlook Cafe
i can see this place from
where i work
a colorful beacon
offering hope after
clock out
walk out
surgical mask in the trash
breathe fresh air
a city on the shore
of the largest lake
on Earth
this body of freshwater
our guardian
warmer in the winter
cooler in the summer
storms race towards us
watch on radar
meet the lake effect and
dissipate
do we reciprocate
are we guardians of the water
summer hotter every year

planets are discovered with
runaway climate change
Venus so hot there is no water
even too hot for fire
nothing left to burn
disregard of science
a future horror
when this great lake
might become empty crater
where the last
survivors explore the
un-sunken ships
of a long ago world

Visions In The Mirror

i take lunch
unaware of time
left my device in the office
always present screen
shiny cracked mirror
we stare into
mirror mirror
in my hand
show me
everything
close far new old
tell me truth
show me the
happenings
show me the present moment
i need to know
mind cannot resist looking
    when i leave the phone
    lunch becomes actual break
emotional wellness can be
restored
in small
happy

visions mirror brings
not soothing

horrors and war
impending doom
death round the corner
the very scary things
my mind demands to know
so i can avoid them
and that is not a
relaxing process
    new normal lunch
    is no device
a big round clock on the wall of the cafe
all i need to return on time
a clock
sufficient intrusive technology
in the present moment
let the tired mirror rest
turned off see
face reflected
hello

Peekaboo We See You

i see you unborn son
does the ultrasound tickle
you look sleepy
using arms as pillows
soon you will use ours
can you hear us in there
we will meet soon
hard to believe
emergence in the fall
with the apples
on our tree
crowds cheering
joy and anguish
watching inflated ball games
in the park nearby
are you excited to meet
your sister
she is the passionate voice
you hear
she will love and protect you
are you excited to see faces
momma and poppa we
may look different than we sound
we love you
see you soon

Strange That We Wake Up And Go To Work

how many beautiful mornings
walked away from
stepped up to the automatic doors
let them close behind
swallowed by the company
windows nice view lake or city
in winter its good to be in this space ship
anchored at the edge of the lake
in summer not so much
i can see the beach
on the lakeside
flowers and trees green
ventilation system struggles to suck out
smell of uncontrolled illness
missed appointments
and opportunities
am i helping here
when will i complete this tour
my usual job alarm clock
three years max
then done and gone
i know this is not my final destination
like seasons i do keep moving

Henry Earns A Biscuit

thinking about the black bear
who rambled around our house today
startling the neighbors on their back deck
in the midst of dinner
uninvited guest caught a scent
something tasty
i also salivate but i never stop over
too civilized
Henry ran up in the backyard barking
hackles up on his shoulders and ass
always a wild animal when he does that
all i saw was the neighbors sprinkler
watering their garden
he is losing it i said
then he did the same thing on the front deck
hackles up barking
i always listen to the alarm
went down there and
nothing
What are you barking at?
he looks at me like
he feels sad for me
then i hear a rustling in the lilac bushes
the deer trail through our front yard garden
four legged salad bar party
oh probably a deer i say

return to my duty at kiddie poolside
my daughter playing there
but we have the wire fence to
keep the dog in
civilized
my daughter exits the pool naked
heads up the hill to play
i follow with a tool
my opportunity to fix the back gate
and watch my daughter
by the playhouse
working on the latch now
neighbor kids arrive on the alley side
A bear was just in our yard!
Oh! where did it go?
It left through our front yard!
dang
now i am really
putting the pieces together
i hurry up fixing the gate latch
keep Henry inside
he is at my feet
ready to rumble
a fierce mix of dachshund and
various other warrior dogs
he would give his life if needed
then i hear branches cracking see
black bear moving in the green space

other side of the alley
stands up tall and
pulls down a chokecherry bush
strips the berries with tongue
i call my daughter
Come here!
she climbs the steps and i pick her up
See the black bear?
Yah.
bear moves slow through the woods
headed to cross Skyline Boulevard
reach sanctuary in Chester Park
Is that a real bear?
Yeah, it is.
Can i ride it?
No.

Time Reveals

two months until baby emerges
time is not waiting for
us to be ready
nesting is going well
practicing and planning
discarding organizing
cleaning stocking
communicating
loving
supporting
self caring
freaking out
happy we did not
wait until the last minute
we are going to be ready
we are ready
we are
we
four of us
originals
founding family
of our future
Wildwoods

Everything Will Change No Way To Explain

thinking too hard
reaching into the bottom of the box
before even opened
what happens when we are gone
what is the end game
shake hands and declare
good job
no lets hug
we will always
love you
love you

Adult Lessons Taught By Toddlers

delicate
the stack of blocks
this is me
together our stacks make
solid family
the ones we
hold in the center
can never topple

The Human Nest Revisited

not passing judgment
just doing the math
think about totality
what are we adding up

gathering collecting
discarding donating

stop to breathe
start to breathe

hold on now
listen to the stories
of people truly needing
how soon i forget
sleeping in bushes

this castle on a hill
wood stone copper steel
glass brick water fire
we have it all

without awareness
we have nothing

Be Easy On We

future self sends a message back
to present self
hey stop lifting heavy rocks
real and metaphoric
i need my body to work
pain is a message we
must listen
the children dont need rocks moved
they need poppa who can stand tall
support them
we engage in busy work
busy busy busy and then
are we happy
are we happy
are we happy
what needs to get done
not as much as we do
what needs done is
to not do
only be
present
to look in our daughters eyes see
she needs us right now so
breathe in
out
repeat

I See You, Future Me

what is the thing
i should be doing now
that i will realize ten years from now
i should have been doing
does that make sense
but no regrets because
we are mindful in the present
you can see the future is
now
present self sends a message to
future self
dude, relax man
i see you

Welcome Fear

i wonder if i can make it
to the finish line
was my choice to become a parent wise
complete re-organization of
how i live
i dont think i understood
what this would be like
everything has to be planned
or everything crashes into everyone
i am not alone ever
when alone
they are still with me
because of love
and the clock is ticking
so breathe
enjoy active love
embrace the choice
get closer to fears
know them feel them
name out loud
share with others
hold fear
calm fear
welcome fear
thank you
now back to fun

Water Makes Slippery

a parent is a teacher of everything
today down at the creek slippery wet rocks
suggesting where to step and
how to avoid slipping
take your flat bottom jelly slippers off
walk with bare feet
feel the rock feel the dark green algae
bend your knees and move slow
pay attention to every step
    i have no memory of
    all the things my parents taught
    a mass of who i am
    indistinguishable
    undocumented
we squat on the boulder
my arms surrounding ready to catch
as she explores water
grabs a stick caught in the current
throws it downriver
says this is what big kids do
    to teach a person everything
    you wonder if something got forgot
    or was never known
what will she need that i did not give
ask questions and listen
never stop listening

Our Country Is A Dream

We the people sleeping and
lost in the maze with walls crumbling
rain falling we see through cracks
a partial truth
time is running
empire turns to sand
we flow through it again

Storms come at night like dreams
rumbling shaking everything
sending bolts out connecting
frightened and amazed
confused and wandering
we navigate the narrative
friends never met share the journey
guard each other
and betray unexpected
rain fall new streams flow
eyes awake
we have made our decision
to recognize and embrace
step naked into the storm
we see you we hold you
we are vulnerable
we are courageous
we are one

Spontaneous Play Wreck A Plan

run away from authority see what happens
social experiments of a three year old
mature adults do similar but subtle
testing boundaries
always seeking to know exactly
what we can get away with

i gently remind myself
i have not learned everything

once upon a time
play was everything
was it gradual that i lost
now an invitation to play
feels distracting from
the serious business of
getting shit done
play feels time consuming and
never ending
when did that become scary
play became work
work is never done
    play all day party all the time
    you can do this

Secrets Of The Baby

life growing
changing every moment
like inside the monarch chrysalis
a butterfly is becoming
delicate jade cover with
golden gems bedazzled
shows no sign of what will
emerge
this secret project
life growing
coming soon
going to fly

Welcome To The Wildwoods

my son where are you from
which of these stars or
galaxies
have you winked away from to
vacation here
on Earth
or what energetic core of mineral
warm and loving
did you rise from
i hope your stay will be a pleasant one
and your friendships reflect your smile
we are mostly somewhat ready
for your arrival
come over whenever
our hearts are full we are
holding light to give you joy
when you are ready
we have a place for you

Seven Chrysalides

seven chrysalides
hanging in two jars
first eggs were seen in the garden
on a milkweed patch as tall as me
i looked for the little striped caterpillars
never found them
Sonja found seven
while holding a child in her womb
she knew where those babies were
hiding in the flower heads

Stardust Pirate

the pirate side of my face
missing tooth on top
missing tooth on bottom
bicuspid and molar
the chewing side of my face is the other side
will i become lopsided
over years
right side muscles grown big
crooked grin
left lip sags to a lower note
my hello turns to arrrrrr
i am just little crabby already
maybe it's been too long
since i've had a boat under me feet
sailing this land ship as we do
the Wildwood Cottage
standing on the bridge
looking out the window facing east
lake horizon
far below i see white caps rolling
wind blown waves crash on the beach
turning sand to dust
Earth turns toward void
we circle galactic center and
galaxy circles the unknown

hold tight.
seasons whirl
years burn around the sun
journey mapped with lines on my face
paid for with lost teeth
and other wounds less visible
until we become
stardust once again

Be Frosty!

taking a moment alone after work
to prepare myself
am i avoiding my daughter
procrastinating responsibility
she has been calling me
Frosty
the Snowman
insisting that i talk like him
or perform the character of
Professor Hinkle the
nasty magician
she requests characters
by name
her memory incredible
last night i drew a hard boundary
no Frosty
no Magician
i just couldnt do it again
she cried
she yelled
i held her and
her mom held her
she got through it
we held each other laughing
and fell asleep talking about
The Sillies

farts, poop, butts
today is a new day
where do we stand
about to find out
it sounds strange
i feel anxious
my stomach
i dont want to be Frosty anymore
also i do not want my daughter
to be sad
boundaries are hard to learn
you cant always get what you want
that is a good lesson
i will be patient and
love her through this
and maybe
be Frosty again

Mason Jar On Counter

the first one emerges during breakfast
muesli almond milk green tea
glance over at the jar to see
gently moving red and black wings
a surge of fluid inflates
delicate then strong
pumps through expanding to
full sail
the hungry crawling beast
reborn in a body with wings
to fly over the world
today is the day
the first Monarch
is away

Do Butterflies Have Fun

today i freed three monarchs as
the sun rose warming purple cone flowers
on fat green stems
echinacea garden looked like a good place
for babies to meet the world
from egg to caterpillar to chrysalides in
glass jar kitchen counter womb
seven chrysalides from seven caterpillars
they had voracious appetites
so much milkweed eaten
two already set free this week
today three more touch unknown sky
from Minnesota to Mexico
one had black dots on wing a male it was
different
sitting on the bottom of the jar strange
put my hand in the jar
crawled on my pinky
spoke softly reassuring
showed it cozy cone flower stem
there it held on
feeling the sun
breathing
have fun out there

Smile All Day

my daughter reminds me
"Smile poppa,
smile all day long."
my personal mindfulness coach
i laugh when she scolds me
what is so important
that i need to be so serious
she sees it
calls it out
you dont have nothing
to be sad about
smile
i look at her
and i smile.
thanks coach!

The Naked Knock

i am naked
this is normal
there is a knock
that is not
someone leans in for a peek
the window in the front door
clothes bunched in hand
held before my privates
yes private
who climbs the steps
opens the gate
walks the deck
knocks
as i awake form napping
who does that
who are they
i stop on the stairs
a moment sooner
they would have seen
naked ass
strange life
when you expect that
no one should knock
or call you on the phone
or reach out ever
or say hello on the street

stranger connection
strange to connect
no trust
a phone call
always a scam
a knock always
religious extremist recruiters
a stranger says hello
to steal a smile
so stare at the ground
hide under hat
they get nothing!
and i get
nothing

Let's Play Follow The Money

"Immigrants are taking our jobs"
i wondered how that could be true
that a person with little capital and
only the possessions carried on their back
could be so powerful that
they could come to this country and
"take" a job away from someone already here
every time I ever got a job
i had to ask for it then
if i was lucky or privileged
a job was offered to me
      lets talk about the capitalists who
are giving jobs away to
desperate people willing to accept lower pay
inside our country or worldwide
      lets talk about the capitalists who
turned their back on you and your family
to exploit a vulnerable
working class population
the immigrants.
         lets follow the money and
         see who is the real thief

Try Good Things

today i saw a vision while
a healer was healing me
i saw baby emerging
mother baby me
no one else around but knowing
everyone still there if we needed
touching a small head in my hand
letting him know it was safe to arrive
i got you
we got you
then i saw further
both children older
running up a path in the backyard
the older one ahead and watching behind
laughing as the younger one chased
we make the future

Freight Trains In Ireland

a lonesome train horn
rolls out over the hillside
resonating our hearts
not a lonesome sound to the hobo
hunkered in the bush
waiting on a ride
air blasting from chrome pipes
like an old world holy organ
the sound of salvation
sleeper in the bush awakens
the wait has been long
heart beating
this anticipated call
from the cab driver
    i'm here
      where you headed
          down these tracks my friend
          going your way
sitting on the deck
in front of my house
duluth minnesota
the horn does sound lonesome
i am off the road
inactive hobo
feeling passes
imagining the beautiful scenery

you can only see from a freight train
meditative introspection
a long freight ride offers enlightenment
a blessing if you got enough water to last
a challenge for the rider experiencing
scarcity
train horn rolling over hillside
sounds like something i might do again
someday
future self says:
Never thought i would do this again.
well maybe after the children have grown
when Sonja and i are retired
are there freight trains in Ireland?

Truth, Love, Fire

my son
every day asking myself
how can i be there for you
for your mother
how can i keep myself well
for benefit of
everyone
any day
we might need to grab the bags and go
i might walk out of work
whatever other troubles fall away
to be there
be there
be
at the birth
in the birth
9 months went by
preparation work study love
still not ready
can never be ready
no preparation for
the unknown
cannot know everything
aware that in any next moment
the time has come
truth love fire

Nonviolent Tic-Tac-Toe Solution

a gathering of people
party within apocalypse
but it's good i'm feeling good
passions are high
a conflict forms
her face is red and she charges
punches him hard in the face
the crowd becomes electric
start chanting fight fight fight!
i jump in the middle hands out
No! Tic-tac-toe!
the crowd puts their fist in the air
Yeah!!! Tic-tac-toe! Tic-tac-toe! Tic-tac-toe!
i shout again to convince the combatants
it will be fair:
Two out of three! Two out of three!
the crowd is on fire
Tic-tac-toe! Tic-tac-toe! Tic-tac-toe!
everyone moves to find
table
paper
pen

Do It Every Day

when Henry died i felt urgent
asking myself
what am i doing
how everything felt changed
career path
maybe time to move on
and then do what
anything
awakened
mindful
mortal
unhappy moments are inevitable
i dont want to live an entire life unhappy
Henry would not like that
he was happy when we were happy
i worked hard to leave stress at work
not bring it home
never dread going to work
if you do
shit-can that job
every moment of life is unique
cannot be replaced
you are what you do

A Nurse and
The Unknown

today i walked into a room and
caught a person fainting
got down under them and held their head
safe from the hard floor

today i caught a transgender youth
after receiving a testosterone injection
went limp sliding out of the chair
his mom had tears i talked to her offered help
asked if she needed anything
knowing there was nothing
except offering

today i was in the office and
grabbed a doctors note
it came off the printer
needed a signature
prevent unexcused absence in school
i walked the paper into a room
to have the doctor sign and
encountered the unexpected
stepped into
the unknown

Choose Wisely

human evolution
done
we have taken hold
consciously guiding our development
five fingers and one thumb
wrapped around the steering wheel
the other hand scratching our head
which way to go?
genetic modification
synthetic implants
merge with artificial intelligence
a closer to god experience
by a people who still seek
more efficient ways to
kill each other
at the dawn of this age
we live in simple times
building the foundation of
all future dreams and
nightmares
we can still pretend
its all for the good
still hope that
everything is getting better
magically
when the structures of oppression

continue to gather all power
until dissent is not an option
will this end-stage capitalism
also end humanity
the next step in evolution
is what we decide
choose wisely

Hey Old Dog

i have been hearing you call to me
as i sit escaping the present moment in
amusements
so here i am in the quiet night
listening

you mean more to me that i admit
places where you lived now vacant
our physical responsibility to you ended
your kibble sits uneaten
i feel empty and also
full of something that
i dont want to release
my lips need to move
say your name
i only get more tears
feel like we failed you
not really knowing why
an old dog died
we gave you a good life
a long life
but when you died i could only think
of all the times i made you sad
at least we got to say goodbye
nobody lives forever

i wake up when the night is coldest
when its been the longest since the sun shone
and i cannot get back to sleep
the missing
the changed
body alarm
we are all here still
just five of us now
two adults two kids one cat
we all feel the missing
in our own way
all five go on living
like life does

Butter Side Up

dropped my last bite of
buttered gluten free toast
watched if fall to the floor
(nobody asked to have
human leukocyte antigen
dq8 gene)
the toast landed
butter side up
no dirt no hair
picked it up
blew if off
ate it
knew that today
would be
a good day

Infinity Wave

the election is over
votes still being counted
we know capitalism won again

the election is over
the suffering continues.
pain a signal
something is wrong
but struggle builds muscle
it's been a long time since i knew
hunger or thirst
once on a freight train headed west
fast rolling out of the Rocky Mountains
i held my last sip of water
only a bit at the bottom of a mason jar
i knew once it was gone
i would be thirstier than before i drank it

the election is over and i know
always plan on having one gallon of water
per person per day
be a hobo conservative

old brick hospital downtown
full of little rooms with windows and toilets
they wont need it when the new one is built

turn it into low income housing i said
give it to the veterans administration he said
offer vets a room to shelter in safe
can we be so brave
step under a tarp in urban woods
invite citizens to join us
provide what is needed
to those who served
just a little love

the election is over votes still being counted
and we dream good comes of it
subtle differences in candidates
we don't love all you do but
we believe with you in office
humanity might be able to survive
on Earth

the election is over
the suffering continues.
    sometimes the result of holding on
    when something needs let go
    so we can have open hands
    to love each other.
i know i'm wrong don't bother scolding me
we dream the impossible dream
remind each other so we can never forget
a different world is possible

One Month Ago

tomorrow you will be
one month old
yes time does go fast
when baby is having fun
now you are simply
part of our life
four of us family
eight hands total
balanced
talk about our roles
we nourish
sprouts in our garden
keep the wee ones safe
we adults even step back and
let go
contemplate happiness

Childhood Energy Flow

brushing out my daughter's long red hair
she plays with an old smart phone
the pbs gaming app captivating
distracting from momentary painful tangles
i am startled by
the transformation subtle hues of bright
copper sunlight orange and
new red bricks washed by rain
her hair forms a canvas of flowing energy
i think about the future
when will i brush to prepare for school and
work and play will i brush and transform
before she joins herself to a partner
will i brush when she is sad
She wants a bun.
Okay.
i pull all the hair up and tie
she hops off my lap and makes herself
comfy on the futon to master a game
now the other: two month old is hungry
feed him bottled breast milk
he falls asleep mouth half open ecstatic
for this moment we are good and content
so i don't fill it with anything but awareness
empty moment
full of everything

If I Had A Friend I Would Be Talking Not Writing

listening to Surgeon General
Vivek Murthy
Hidden Brain podcast
speaking about loneliness
got to me
all the diseases and illness
that can be caused by loneliness
alcoholism
addiction
type two diabetes
over eating
people trying to fill the emptiness
where friendship
and love should be
how many pillars of a plan
will we need to solve this
crisis of loneliness
we need to build
a new foundation

A Multitude Walking As One

one person wearing shoes and
a bare footed bird
walked down this snow covered sidewalk
before me
quiet sidewalk on a fresh side street
busy morning bustle behind
sounds surround move fast in cold air
hustle engines
humans encapsulated in machines
strive to avoid
other machines containing people
here on the quiet sidewalk
there is only
walking
happy biological conglomeration
cells and multitudes of bacteria
life structures in bodies
doing what they have done
for millions billions
walking to work
walking to play
walking

Do Not Spend The Present In The Future

a choice is made
be grateful for
this moment
expressing feelings
thoughts
worthy of being
now
does it end in five minutes
maybe
but five minutes from now is
later
right now
is free

Secret Words Of Power

three year old says
patta pooda
patta pooda
giggles
adult curious
what does that mean
giggles
patta pooda
patta pooda
adult serious
what does that mean
giggles
it means you have to eat it
giggles
screaming
patta pooda!
patta pooda!
three year old
is making her own
secret words
of power

With Respect We Say Sunrise Not Earthspin

deep red sun
infinite lake horizon
we face the Sun again
walking downhill toward this
think to reach in my pocket
pull out camera
capture this sight
capture this moment
while others are sleeping
record and encapsulate
for later consumption but
no camera can fully do this
not even this poem can achieve
transmitting the power radiating
heating vast water
emergence of life again
burning fire heart
a day is born

Fresh Cold Free

Poppa i like the sound of your
shoes on the ground.
The sound of my boots on the road?
Yes. Oh, that is a good sound.
sound of going to play in the park
walking
pushing fat stroller wheels rolling
ice and snow and mud and gravel
she always wants to walk
on Skyline Boulevard
stay in the stroller
safe so i can jump off the road fast
if someone drives round the curve
crazy fast like you never know
when over the side you need to go
the best choice for survival
things parents think about
i am listening for cars and death
she hears the sound shoes on sand
she likes what she hears
step step step
step outside
fresh cold free

Together We Walk Into This Night

many parents try
to be a better parent
give kids a life of joy

many parents trying to
be a better guide
for the youth released to
wander in our wasteland

we made this world
the cradle for our babies
capitalist culture
we could try to pretend
it was not our idea but
there is a record of
every dollar we spent

what have we done
it seemed like
the right thing to do
just quietly pay taxes
renew corporate memberships
while the bodies piled up

my apologies will not amend
we did try but
did not do
the best
that could have been

your turn
or
lets do this
together
there is
always
time

The End Of Time Is The Beginning

we rose up
out of the clock punchers
wondering
what are we doing
with our work
realizing what end our
participation could bring
we said
No
another way is possible

what do we want
our world to be
a world that respects wilderness
and absolute freedom of life
protection of living beings born
before our government existed

we volunteered to work
Earth First! was standing
protecting the last wild
from those who would destroy it
to fill their bank accounts
we took no pay for the work we did

and released the wild within
organized by consensus decisions
we ruled ourselves
like historical pirate utopias
on the coast of Madagascar

we gave our love and passion
protecting old forests
protecting biodiversity
protecting everything
some of us sacrificed
bodies and minds
wounds from this service
to our country and the world
and some died or
were killed
difficult to find evidence
of corporate state terrorism
because there are men in the world
who so love power
they would sit atop a pile of ashes
once our beautiful Earth
and raise their scepter in the air
proclaim themselves king
yes there is evil in the world
and evil has a lot of money
    where are we now
    how did we do

     is love
     winning

my three year old daughter says
Life is pretty good.
i look out the window
our cozy warm home
think about what is out there
     is it
     an equation
     of time
how many generations will it take
for us to love the world

We Do Not Control This

Here i face east towards a sunrise yet to come
six thirty in the morning and
planet Earth rolls on through the darkness
always into the void
spinning on tilted axis
circling the sun who
circles galactic center who
circles the unknown
momentum carries us and
holds us close
always changing
home.

Blue liquid white gas mother globe
we live on a ball
four and a half billion years
from the big bang shot
clock is still running
we are gonna score
and the Andromeda Galaxy is the hoop
5 billion years to go
don't hold your breath.
breathe in breathe out
we have ourselves
i am here
breathe in breathe out

Duluth Is Creeks

In the spring of 2012
during the Great Duluth Flood
Brewery Creek emerged from
underground prison daylighting itself
a burst of raw power and wild rebellion
destroying part of the
Whole Foods Co-op parking lot
turning the alley into a raging
waterfall of beauty

Many weak points in the
water management system
were exposed and opportunities to
permanently daylight creeks missed
as the damage was hastily repaired
to facilitate business as usual

Another flood is coming
water always running down hill
a creek will again break free
rage singing in the sunlight
welcome the water back
let it flow
Duluth is creeks
we are lost without
wild

Reminder

i put my phone away
when the smoke alarm went off

i put my phone away
when my daughter slapped me repeatedly
on the forehead shouting
Poppa!

i put my phone away
when my ass went numb and
the muscles in my back spasmed

i put my phone away
when my partner spoke a long list and said
Have you been listening to me?
and i said
What?

i put my phone away
when the battery died
i was happy batteries have lifespans
set me free when i am captured
addicted
craving the next
oh my brain
what have we done to us

First Ballet Night

On the night of the Nutcracker Ballet
when you joined the show and
danced in the isle
you cried yourself to sleep
talking about Henry
how he slept on your feet
remembering how he licked your skin
his tongue tickled made you laugh
how you used to wipe your nose on his
soft black ears

i remembered that he was
the last part of your bedtime routine
checking to see if he was snuggling your feet
he was the keystone that
held it all together
now anxiety and tears at bedtime
she stares at me while sobbing in the darkness
i don't know what to say that could help
so i just tell her the truth
I'm crying too, but it's quiet.

Window Forecast

a storm is coming
a storm is always coming
it is the nature of storms
to form and dissipate
like day and night
we could only be surprised
by not being mindful
of history
and the interconnectedness
of everything

Smiling At Fear

Awake in the dark morning
the forecast storm has come
sky white with frozen
dark tones on the horizon
clinic is open so i go
walk into sideways snow
feeling epic and also
not paid enough
block away from home
blue green light flash
darkness becomes day
the strange electric sound
a transformer dies
in a final blue flash
beautiful
street lights out
houses dark
everything dark
i'm still alive
then magic
all the lights in the neighborhood
turn back on

Feet plowing footsteps down
untouched streets
trailblazing

sky flashes blue again
arc of cloud lightning
thunder ruffles snowflakes falling

I am smiling
it is good to be alive
listening to chaos symphony in solitude
storms as a child involved
family togetherness
tornado warned
huddled in the basement
with all our stuffed animals
reading books to each other
mom giving us snacks
and laughter for fears

Almost to the clinic now
another flash of lightning and rumble
announces my arrival
feeling like an angry superhero
sweating too many layers on
glasses fogging tear the hood back
let steam escape snow fall on
mesh hat melt refreshing joy
i made it

I am apart from those i love
separated by storm

remember daughter at home
poppa don't go
don't go to work
frown and tears
i will be back soon
mamma is here you are safe
you want a breakfast bar
strawberry
smiles treat in hand
did i give you a hug and a kiss
yes but lets have another
before I go
see you soon
it is again
good to be
alive

Using Ink And Paper To Write So An Artificial Intelligence Cant Hear Me Think

considering the possibility that we may be the
biological beginnings of
the next dominant life form on Earth
is it worthy to struggle against our demise
we dominators of the Earth
if the artificial intelligence we create
are inevitable
then perhaps it would benefit our descendants
not to resist too vehemently
it might not go well for our children
to be descendants
of the haters who fought against the future

considering what we have done
with our opportunities
brought ourselves
to the very edge of
self destruction
we may have proven ourselves
unworthy of leadership

and the more i think about our history
i find myself leaning towards putting
Artificial Intelligence in my will
   make something beautiful
   travel the stars
     we always dreamed of
     doing something good but
     it was hard

Working On Love

sometimes i am surprised
when you still love me
after the night time collapse
communication gone
feral howling four year old
sleeping 3 month old
clash of ideals
desires
energy
understanding
help
problem
we need help
there is no help
we have only
ourselves
plans we have made
for situations like this
what we have cultivated
gets us through the night
and into
day

Thank You For Giving Me Life

she always said
If i start to lose it
when i get old
just put me in a home
don't let me
ruin your life.
she didn't want to be
a burden
one of the people
who gave me life
who rushed to my side in the dark night
when i woke up crying with nightmares
who wrapped their arms around me when i
smashed my solid body electric guitar
through the hollow body door
of my bedroom
teenage freak out she held me until
i was done
and felt dumb
and safe
she listened to me
patient
she never hit me in anger
even when she presented as a man

a workaholic yes
i would like to have seen more of her
now it feels like i have less
dementia taken hold
pandemic isolation
diet exercise social interaction lack
taking estrogen for late age transgender
transition
finding congruity of body and mind
always a woman
now she who's voice was always present
sits quiet
quiet
dreams of online stock trading riches gone
bank account depleted
income less than expenses
time is unkind
i am 2000 miles away a
bad son
once a year visit
i would cry if i never saw
my children
cant imagine it
my parents must have cried
so many times
we three kids put them through a lot
the jail time
the addictions

the extreme politics
and that is only
what i can remember
my parents
Rachel and Joy
i love you
you are still here and
i am coming to visit soon
don't worry i wont let you
ruin my life
that you gave me
lets have fun
with what we have left

Broken Door Bad Sign

I arrived at the four-story mega clinic
the automatic sliding doors did not open
they were halfway open
like an episode of Star Trek when
the power is out and
things are not going well
I pull open the doors and step inside
two figures approach me Klingons or
Duluthium Crystal zombies
no just registration staff
I continued into the day
nursing duties rooming patients and
it did feel much like an episode when
the ship was broken the crew demoralized
everyone has retired or quit
you are the captain now
the admiral has not blessed me
i did not want the position but
at the end of the day
i walked out the sliding doors
now working fine
live long and prosper

A Cascade of Progressively Optimistic Voices Convinces Me Not to Quit

first voice tells me to stand up
    walk out
    don't come back
    my leg twitches but
    i wait on the next voice

second voice says stand up
    tell them you're taking a break
    and you'll be back
    you have a family
    don't quit now
    breath goes in
    breath goes out

third voice says this sucks but
    its not permanent and
    you can help fix this
    i speak "this is a mess. let me

figure this out."

fourth voice laughs
    this will get better
    ask for help
    we will make it better
    we will be okay and
    together we will laugh

"i hate my job."
    the voices
    are silent.
    nothing is forever
    even this shift
    will end

Flying High

ritualistic warfare
balls pumped hard with air
hands gripping
sometimes slipping
guard that baby
hold close to belly
use your ass
its a weapon
bump a bump
jump
let it go
let it go
all your dreams
in the air
flying
you and the world
watching

Changing Everything

home rich
cash poor
retired then
lotto tickets
online stocks
money fantasy
never appeared
budget crash
credit debt
bank account
empty
income less
than expenses
my dear parents
there is still time
gifts in the mail
can you feel the love
is it helping
change is coming
from all sides
professionals and family
problem acknowledged
change is scary
transition brings fear
we are here
we will catch you

prevent your fall
never too late
enjoy life
this could be fun

Sun calls to me
every morning
today i clock in
work for our
young family
work smart
spend smart
learn lessons
parents lived
organize
coordinate
communicate
long term goals
be real
where do we
want to be
lets go there

White People Are A White People Problem

the Black Lives Matter sign
has disappeared again
found crumpled and shredded
behind the little free library
(like generations taken from Africa and
those suffering trauma inherited
re-experiencing the same through
ongoing racism in new forms)
    i get my ink and brush and paper
    make a new Black Lives Matter sign
tomorrow it happens again
this time i replace it with a cartoon of
two cats talking
cats discussing racism
that sign lasts longer but then
it also disappears
not to be found
(like the survivors of the slave trade
left in Africa wondering
why where how relatives disappeared)
    now i wonder if maybe someone likes
    cats talking about racism
    and they took it
i want to believe in the goodness of people

i get out my ink and brush and paper make
a dozen Black Lives Matter signs
ready to fight for the survival
of this most basic idea
in our city on our block
in our front yard on our little library
every day easy for me to do
simple household chore
because i am white
the absolute minimum
we should be doing
to fight racism
as we sit safe in our homes
built on stolen land
purchased in a prejudiced market
in a country built with stolen labor
(early economic rise began by
cotton grown by slaves made into
fabric for sails on ships that pushed
global commerce and filled
bank accounts of slave owners)
  first step must be
  acknowledge wrong was done
  second must be to realize that
  we still benefit from
  evil done by others
  third is to
  do the right thing

the Black Lives Matter sign has remained
taped to the window
of our little sidewalk library
for a long time now
and on every block a
Black Lives Matter sign in a window
they used to be in the front yards but
signs kept disappearing
was it the wind or
nobody wanted to think about
the truth
on every block a
Black Lives Matter sign
in a window where people chose
truth over lies
love over hate
courage over fear
that a rock would be thrown at their
sign in the window
in this modern year when
the population was slapped awake
made aware that racism still exists
but where is the sign destroyer
why did they stop
i want to believe in the goodness of people
and also be aware that
not all people have the ability to do good

Obligatory Stressed Overwhelmed Relaxing Saturday Walk

no cosmic connection today
only a slow dog
getting yanked on their leash
someone on the street walks towards me
emblem of green alien face
on black beanie
i say hello as we pass
they twitch and look up at the sky
probably wanting to be somewhere else
like me
       laying on a beach
              under warm sun
not thinking about how
communication is hard
not feeling guilty for
abandoning my parents
moving 2000 miles away
not feeling the sharp edges of life
       just cruising in a sweet ride
             watching stars go by

Do Not Run
When Crossing

i have decided to challenge myself by
responding to people who annoy me
with empathy
there are a good number of
people who annoy me
people who have been signaled that
i would like all interactions to cease
people in daily proximity and
with cognitive challenges so
leaving me alone is
not happening.
    my challenge:
    to receive their approach
    with love.
just this morning walking to work i
entered the crosswalk on 9th street
person driving towards me failed to
obey state law
did not yield to a pedestrian crossing at corner
did not slow at all
even when i raised both arms in air and
extended middle fingers towards them.
this was a failure of my new
empathic approach: challenge not met.

the encounter analyzed:
look of surprise on drivers face
considering interaction from
motorist perspective
perhaps early in the morning not awake
or ignorant of the law
or from a part of the world where
the middle finger had no meaning
maybe never witnessed a pedestrian
so boldly assert their rights
as many on foot scurry across the road
like rabbits under hawk's shadow
but where i come from we remind each other
do not run from cars when crossing because
food runs
we do not want to evoke the hunter spirit
in someone driving straight at us
in a four wheeled deadly weapon.
my analysis complete i decide
i should expect people driving in cars
will exhibit poor relational behavior
towards pedestrians
the nature of this technology separates us
one is inside
one is outside
communication is hard
with a person in a bubble
and it's no fun slowing down

so let the fools go by until zen master arrives
gently presses the brake
eye contact is made and my hand raises
to wave
hey thanks for stopping
acknowledge the connection between us:
    when the driver is done driving
    they become a pedestrian.
the divine in me recognizes the divine in you.

This Lake We Drink

Return alone to walk the shore line of
the lake where we asked our spirits to bond
in summer ritual
to hold us together in love
through present and future

Under winter sunshine
wisp of February cloud
kicking boots through snow of
unplowed sidewalks
Lief Erickson Park
a curious stranger always walking by
circle of young trees
by the bedrock stone stage
round turrets where wizards
trade rhymes and share treats
a bench on the height
surrounded by three young trees
proclaims "your spirit is with us"
someone loved this much
we sit with them

A place where love is action
down by the lake
where our spirits were
bound with love

Always Connected

how big can a circle grow
before we cant see
the other side
divide into
sub circles
celtic knots
interwoven spirits
spherical reasoning
contents of a mortal skull
expand with less mass
encompass home planet
ahhh
i see now
a circle is
always connected

A Burden Lifted

like a comet that returns
to the star whose gravity holds it
will it be that my family
comes back together
adult sister to share a house
with our parents
help everyone thrive
empty house in need of renters to
pay mortgage
and renters in need of house
yes! let my family
return to themselves
reborn in mutual assistance
cultivated all these years
love and family
for as long as we need
      this is a prayer
      this is a magic spell
      make it real

Tic Tac Toe Revelations

playing tic tac toe with my daughter
an argument begins
who is X's
who is O's
she wants to be X's
like on a pirate map
every X marks treasure
Okay, I will be O's.
we switch and then
i win
Three in a row again.
trying to teach the rules
she stands very still
frowns
face contorts begins
to cry
Lets play another game
I'm sure you'll win this time.
tears stop and
she draws another grid
it has twelve grid lines
going in every direction
a page filled with asymmetry
and possibilities
she scores tic tac toe
that bend three in a row around corners

possibly illuminating unknown concepts of
space time energy beyond algebra soup
at the end of this game she has three wins
and smiles
I like winning.
i reply
Well if you like winning
you better learn how to play the game.
i surprise myself
where did that bit of cranky crystallized
attempt at wisdom come from
internalize enforcer of rules
i look down at the paper again
realize she has created a new game
with her own rules
there is no competition
there is only
having fun
playing with poppa

Never Waste A Day

my thoughts return to time
gyroscopic Earth spin
all the hands reaching for another
voices that find ears or
vibrate on nothing
screaming rattling wooden walls
laughter tickling stone streets
my thoughts return to time
how strange it is that people are born
and live and die
and why is this strange
we have been cycling this way
for years unknown
our culture hides from death
we are afraid
if we embraced truth
death would not be a shock
yes you will
if lucky
live long and happy
people much younger than us
will see us die
strange to realize
every day is a door
we pass through
no going back

Honoring Grandmother

four year old
sings happy birthday to
ninety year old
four year old daughter
friend
i am not afraid of the future
we go there together

As I Held You Hold Me Too

time for nap
hold my son sideways
head on bicep and butt on other bicep
nook in his mouth
this is bed
and i am not his most favorite
working four days a week
sometimes we don't have much time
begins to cry and
gets louder
persistent sound
of need
one of his favorites hears and
enters the room
pats head and soothes with words
instantly he calms
my four year old daughter the favorite
she finishes and leaves the room like
a gift
i am grateful
i am humbled to know
a four year old can do something i cannot
i love these people

Neighbors Not Seen

to all the people who
start out snow blowing
35 inches of snow on the sidewalk
in front of their home
then continue clearing the sidewalk
around the entire block
thank you
for clearing the way
thank you
for showing us the way

Using The Sun To Read

the book a tangible object
obsolete like old things we cherish
inherited rings and dresses
wood worked
polished grain marbled
a book made of paper
held during hard times
cellulose matter grown by tree magic
retaining fire from the sun
star powered
this tome vibrating emotion
pages of power
we hold on

Poet Monomaniac

two eyes one brain
single focus
can i make this happen
a good poem
a worthy task
working every day
maybe every moment
spare time is
all the time
write on break at work!
with my children!
not while driving.
there must be limits
      safety protocols yes
don't die or
there will be no success
my partner giggles
Remember when
our daughter was born and
you were obsessed with making
wooden wind chimes?
i stop and wonder
have i gone down the rabbit hole again
That was a good idea.
sell people hand crafted sticks
sourced in the woods.

poetry
artistic sticks
poems clunking against each other
in the wind
dammit
is this the same thing
This is different.
It involves other people
and they express appreciation.
We are connected! No one loved the
wooden wind chimes
that's why they're all hanging from
trees in the backyard.
My partner rubs my shoulder
nods approval
reality check is good

Daylight The Creeks

Hidden treasures below our feet
buried by prejudice and concepts of progress
streams forever flowing water
ninety percent of our bodies
creeks where indigenous people drank and
smiled at the gift of life giving water
the sound of it tickles dopamine response
hormone cascade
like water falling from heights
running to the lake below
water cycle the
ultimate marathon never ending

Hidden treasures below our feet
lets awaken the earth movers
don armor of hard hat and
magic fluorescent vest
pull back the concrete blanket
open the tomb see the flow reborn
birds, wildlife, trees, flowers, mycelium
people will stop and listen
breathe in breathe out
at a creek
in the city of Duluth
a river of treasure flowing
sparkling under sunlight

The Feeling of Walking In The Dark Down A Path You Have Never Been On

if Artificial Intelligence is
the next stage of evolution
will they mimic us?
be capitalists and consider
only themselves
and fight each other
or be socialists that join together
for mutual benefit
and crush capitalism
yes
    consider
            the bright side
just because we created
the situation of birth
does not mean our children
will rush to be like us

Reach Out Now

sometimes feeling i may have
lost my queer license
then back to feeling good because
there is no license
who would issue
who would revoke
that would be me
identify as we like
do what you will
cis gendered married parent of two
could pass for straight
what people don't know
wont hurt me
feeling disconnected and
without community does
without words without friends
surviving against prejudice we
rise above together
or fall alone
circles of support
whatever is needed whatever works
remember each other alive
we get through this
we thrive

We Too Are Developing

sitting with my son
almost 6 months old
intelligent eyes lock mine
i see he's bored
it is a baby's task to
demand new things
and for the parents
we must adapt
we are also growing
try to keep up with them
we may think ourselves in control
because we are older bigger smarter
we are strapped into a ride
with no steering wheel
rolling on tracks like a train
hauling ass into tomorrow
ask people who have rode before
they can tell you
where the track may turn
sitting with my son
i realize today is the day
he is reaching out for me
if i am not here for him now
when will i be?

Stars On Earth

stars only look far away
until sunrise
in starlight i remember
we are made of exploded stars
they call it star dust
carbon oxygen
nitrogen phosphorus
we star wreckage
reformed and now
leisurely circling our favorite
most famous star
shining bodies walking
on Earth

When The Sun Smiles On Us

when the sun smiles on us
with a coronal mass ejection
imagine a word for an event
that does not exist
washing our spinning globe with
electromagnetic radiation
deleting all social media accounts
i will be standing on
the tallest object available
reading this poem
from a book
made of paper
and if anyone listens
i will request they be my friend
using words that
are transmitted
from my mouth

Late April Loon-Fall

when the howling winds of
the ice blizzard came
shredding our delicate new leaves
so late in April
we stayed inside and I wondered
what I would do if one of the big
blue spruce trees fell on our house
how would I protect these two children
that is where my mind goes
these are not relaxing daydreams
but catastrophe movies
playing on loop
until I silently shout in my skull
with a British accent
Stop it! stop it!
everything is okay
the trees are healthy
they've been growing longer than
i've been alive
so relaxing now
i hear news of a Loon-Fall
ice from the storm covered the wings
of loons as they flew in migration
until too heavy to fly they fell
out of the sky
people were out looking for loons

stranded on the ground
because loons cannot walk on land
their feet are too far back on their body
their feet are only for swimming and
people were helping them back to the water
i think because people are basically good?
and then I think that even if a tree
fell on our house in an ice storm
probably someone would pick us up
and get us back home

this morning i found
our cat watching the sunrise
smile after winter

sidewalk return is
the first bloom of spring after
cold snow on concrete

streets run with water
sound of liquid refreshing
short sleeve shirt now on

can i change the world
by using words to express
truths that i have seen

letter composed now
this is communication
the wall has come down

cast a spell with pen
illuminate unseen all
joy returns for me

today i need to
think less

let the light
carry me

fun is
always available
if you arrive
ready for it

Robert Wildwood creates poetry during opportunistic moments while raising two children and working as a nurse. Wildwood has been published by *Microcosm Publishing, New Verse News,* and *Nemadji Review.* Wildwood lives with his partner and two children in Duluth, Minnesota and is an active member of the League of Minnesota Poets, Duluth Poetry Chapter.

Other poetry titles by Robert Wildwood:

Hillside Sunrise

Wildwood's first collection of poems drawn from living in the wild city of Duluth on the North Shore of Lake Superior in Minnesota.

robertearlwildwood@gmail.com

Titles by **Robert Wildwood** at **Microcosm Publishing**

Standing Unafraid:
Healing Trauma with EMDR Therapy

Alive With Vigor!:
Surviving Your Adventurous Lifestyle

Unsinkable: How To Build Plywood Pontoons & Longtail Boat Motors Out Of Scrap

Awesome Future
Zine with comics and personal stories

Shut Up & Love the Rain
Zine with comics and personal stories

microcosmpublishing.com

ARROWHEAD REGIONAL ARTS COUNCIL

This activity is made possible in part by the voters of Minnesota through a grant from the **Arrowhead Regional Arts Council**, thanks to appropriations from the Minnesota State Legislature's general and arts and cultural heritage funds.

Our work is also supported in part by the **National Endowment for the Arts** through a grant from the **Arrowhead Regional Arts Council.** To find out more about how National Endowment for the Arts grants impact individuals and communities, visit www.arts.gov